This delightful Fireside book is the latest in a series that have been specially imagined to help grown-ups learn about the world around them. Using large clear type, simple and easy-to-grasp words, frequent repetition, and thoughtful matching of text with pictures, these books should be a great comfort to grown-ups.

The Fireside Grown-up Guides understand that the world is just as confusing to a forty-year-old as it is to a four-year-old. By breaking down the complexity of grown-up life into easy-to-digest nuggets of information, and pairing them with colorful illustrations even a child could understand, the Fireside Grown-up Guides prove that being a grown-up can be as simple as "look and remember."

The publishers gratefully acknowledge assistance provided by Josh Weinstein, Egregius Professor of Reference at Mars University and Reader-in-Residence at Springfield Library, in compiling this book.

THE FIRESIDE GROWN-UP GUIDE TO

MINDFULNESS

by

J. A. HAZELEY, N.S.F.W. and J. P. MORRIS, O.M.G.

Authors of *TV's Fiftiest Great Sausage Moments*

TOUCHSTONE

New York   London   Toronto   Sydney   New Delhi

Mindfulness is the skill
of thinking you are doing
something when you are doing
nothing.

One of the good things about
mindfulness is that you get to
do a lot of sitting down.

Sitting down is good for the
mind because so much positive
energy is stored in the lap.

People who practice mindfulness first find somewhere quiet to sit down.

Alan is sitting down in Idaho.

Sophie is concentrating on her breath. It smells of Funyuns.

She says she has light for breakfast, air for lunch, and love for supper, but Sophie has also secretly had some Funyuns.

Wendell achieves a state of mindfulness by imagining he is floating in a beautiful lake until his mind empties of everyday worries.

Soon he is aware of himself, but no longer worried about money, work, family, or whether he left the faucet on.

Many home insurance policies now cover Acts of Mindfulness.

Anna has emptied her mind and is just listening to the world around her.

She can hear the neighbors arguing, two ambulances, a burglar alarm, a child crying, and the sound of dubstep coming from a detailed Honda Civic.

She is also concentrating on her own feelings, like her cystitis.

People learn a lot about themselves from mindfulness.

Mindfulness has taught Django to live in the moment.

He used to live in the Hamptons.

ALBION

TO Winchester,
ASHUELOT
NASHUA
KEENE and
STATIONS ON THE
FITCHBURG
ROAD!

Mindfulness has taught Leanne to accept things as they are: rubbish, expensive, unfair, and out-of-date every six months.

It has also taught her to accept things like cake.

Leanne likes cake.

"There is more wisdom in a waterfall than there is in a hundred men," says Jake.

Jake is always saying things like this.

His ex-wife's sister calls him Jerk.

Danny is so mindful that he has forgotten where he parked his car.

Alison has been staring at this beautiful tree for five hours.

She was meant to be in the office. Tomorrow she will be fired.

In this way, mindfulness will have solved her work-related stress.

Chris likes to practice loving-kindness meditation. This is when someone thinks of a friend, then sends them love.

Chris finds this easier than bothering to meet his friends or lending them money.

Fleur is on a silent retreat. She likes going on retreat because it takes days and nobody demands anything of her.

Today a guest speaker is giving a silent speech, after which there will be a silent question-and-answer session.

It is all very different from life in the Minneapolis Bureau of Weights and Measures, where Fleur works. The clock there is very noisy.

Thaddeus has been practicing self-realization for five years.

He has come to realize his true self as an air-conditioning engineer.

He does not miss being chairman of the Federal Reserve.

Mia has found a spiritual retreat in Buffalo.

This is a shame, as she was hoping her husband would pay for her to go to Thailand.

You can achieve mindfulness anywhere, simply by filling your mind with images of calm, serenity, or wonder.

By practicing mindfulness, Martin has found inner peace— even though he is being kidnapped by swans.

Robert became a Buddhist because he was interested in dharma.

"Dharma" is a word for cosmic law and order.

Robert is sad. He thought "dharma" was a type of curry.

In ancient times, Guru Bhellend entered a state of mindfulness that lasted thirty-five years.

During this time, he thought about everything.

When he finished, he wrote the answer on a grain of rice.

He never married.

Sometimes life can be too noisy.

Try not speaking for a while.

Let people know what you want with a smile or a frown or by throwing your keys at the back of their heads.

Jane has tried many ways of energizing and detoxing.

She went on a raw food diet, but the chicken upset her tummy.

Then her tutor told her to "be like water." Jane thought this was a good idea.

Now, just like water, she is drunk most lunchtimes.

Todd likes extreme mindfulness.

Today he is emptying his mind on a tightrope high above the Galveston Shrimpworks.

The people on the pleasure cruiser below hope that Todd doesn't empty any other part of his body.

New sorts of mindfulness are popping up all the time. This is aqua mindfulness.

There are now courses for cardio mindfulness, white-rapper mindfulness, honey-roasted mindfulness, micro-mindfulness, and mindlessness.

In mindlessness, you have to beat up your inner total stranger.

Katarina is in love with the earth, but she worries that it does not love her back.

She practices earth mindfulness. She cries for her friend, the earth. Katarina has no real friends.

Tom and Mozart have gone on a rafting retreat in California.

With only a bottle of water and an inspirational haiku, they set out to find their way to a state of intense curiosity and awareness.

They are lost and tired, and Mozart wants to give up and go find some hookers.

Laura tried mindfulness to get in touch with her inner child.

It turns out that Laura's inner child had been prescribed an experimental cough medicine and was having some very vivid dreams.

Poor Laura.

TOUCHSTONE
An Imprint of Simon & Schuster, Inc.
1230 Avenue of the Americas
New York, NY 10020

First Touchstone hardcover edition October 2016

TOUCHSTONE and colophon are registered trademarks of Simon & Schuster, Inc.

For information about special discounts for bulk purchases,
please contact Simon & Schuster Special Sales at 1-866-506-1949
or business@simonandschuster.com.

The Simon & Schuster Speakers Bureau can bring authors to your live event.
For more information or to book an event, contact the Simon & Schuster Speakers Bureau
at 1-866-248-3049 or visit our website at www.simonspeakers.com.

Manufactured in Mexico

1   3   5   7   9   10   8   6   4   2

Library of Congress Cataloging-in-Publication Data

Names: Hazeley, Jason, author. | Morris, Joel (Comedy writer), author.
Title: The Fireside grown-up guide to mindfulness / J.A. Hazeley and J.B. Morris.
Other titles: Ladybird book of mindfulness. | Mindfulness
Description: New York : Touchstone, 2016. | Series: The Fireside grown-up guides
Identifiers: LCCN 2016011238 | ISBN 9781501150753 (hardback)
Subjects: LCSH: Mindfulness (Psychology)--Humor. | BISAC: HUMOR / Form /
Parodies. | BODY, MIND & SPIRIT / Meditation.
Classification: LCC PN6231.M54 H39 2016 | DDC 818/.602--dc23
LC record available at https://lccn.loc.gov/2016011238

ISBN 978-1-5011-5075-3
ISBN 978-1-5011-5076-0 (ebook)

THE ARTISTS

Martin Aitchison
Robert Ayton
John Berry
R. Embleton
Roger Hall
Frank Hampson
Frank Humphris
B. Knight
Jorge Nuñez
G. Robinson
Charles Tunnicliffe
Clive Uptton
Harry Wingfield
Eric Winter
Gerald Witcomb

THE FIRESIDE GROWN-UP GUIDES TO

MINDFULNESS

THE HUSBAND

THE MOM

THE HANGOVER

If you benefited from the Fireside Grown-up Guide in your hand, look for these others wherever produce and ductwork are sold:

THE HANGOVER

Consuming alcohol lowers the body's reserves of vital elements such as iron, potassium, water, and bacon. Every unit of alcohol kills the equivalent of two inches of bacon, which must be replaced the next morning.

THE HUSBAND

The husband knows many things. For example, he knows how many stairs there are, in case he arrives home unable to see them properly.

THE MOM

The mom does not like hearing her own voice. That is because it does not sound like her voice anymore. It sounds like her mom's.